D0645598

SIMPLE PRINCIPLES
TO RAISE A SUCCESSFUL CHILD

Alex A. Lluch

Author of Over 2 Million Books Sold!*

WS Publishing Group
San Diego, California

To my beautiful children Isabel, Emily, and Alexander.
My love for you cannot be described in words.

SIMPLE PRINCIPLES
TO RAISE A SUCCESSFUL CHILD

By Alex A. Lluch

Published by WS Publishing Group
San Diego, California 92119
Copyright © 2007 by WS Publishing Group

Designed by WS Publishing Group:
David Defenbaugh

For Inquiries:
Logon to www. WSPublishingGroup.com
E-mail info@WSPublishingGroup.com

ISBN 13: 978-1-887169-74-5

Printed in China

TABLE OF CONTENTS

INTRODUCTION

Every parent wants the perfect life for their children, yet very few achieve it. These days, parents are competing with powerful societal forces to keep their children on the right track. But in many cases, they're failing.

Despite record governmental spending on drug and alcohol prevention programs, the number of children turning to these harmful and addictive substances remains steady. Television programs depicting teens in sexual situations are the norm. Companies have targeted children as a consumer group and constantly advertise their unhealthy products to our susceptible youth. Even when we do our best to keep our children from these influences, their friends waste no time encouraging our children to get involved in bad habits and wayward values.

Peers, corporations and the media have our children's rapt attention. These three entities are faster, more novel and more exciting than we are. They are also a danger to our children. When our children choose to follow these influences rather than ours, they assume consciously or unconsciously that these outside forces have their best interests in mind. They do not. Television producers strive to gather viewers. Advertisers want to make money.

Parents, on the other hand, are desperate to make sure their children have the happiest, most fulfilled lives possible. Our decisions and actions stem from that one burning desire. This is why I have written *Simple Principles to Raise a Successful Child*. This book gives parents the tools to reassert themselves as their children's primary influence and helps build family bonds strong enough to withstand the negative pressures our children are facing every day.

Reasserting our parental rights and duties is an obligation. Studies prove that children want us to lead them. Children pick parents as role models first, followed by teachers. Sports and Hollywood figures actually trail far behind. Our children want our guidance. We only need to provide it. *Simple Principles to Raise a Successful Child* will show you how to be the role model that deserves admiration, the disciplinarian who wins respect and the loving parent your children will adore.

What is this book about?

This is not a book that scolds parents for not being involved enough. Nor is it a book that stresses how we have to be stricter with our children. Research has shown that the very strict, authoritative parenting style creates children who become either too aggressive or angry, or so passive and anxious that they can barely function in life. There is a much bigger focus on love in these pages than there is on being stern.

"Discipline" means "to teach," not "to scold, control, hurt or force." Teaching means leading children into good behavior while giving them reasons to avoid bad behavior. We lead children into good performance through our own loving words and actions, by spending time with them, explaining our reasoning, keeping them from harmful friends and activities, talking openly and honestly with them, modeling the behaviors we want them to have and by praising them. These are all indications of love.

This book emphasizes the miracle of affection and love. Scientists have proven that affection has remarkable, positive physical effects on the body. It reduces stress levels, as well as heart and breathing rates, increases the brain's serotonin levels (responsible for making us feel good) and helps muscles relax. Research studies have shown that enhanced love and intimacy can double the length of survival in women with metastatic breast cancer. Children respond best to love. Fill your children with love and they will dispense it to their peers, siblings, you and their own children throughout their lives.

If we want to love, comfort, support and discipline our children, we must learn to slow down. Many parents feel that they are failing in this area. The biggest obstacle, they claim, is not having the time to invest in this process.

It is no secret that children of all ages love and long to spend time with their parents. Most parents know this but don't do anything about it. We're all rushed between balancing work, day-to-day household chores and family life. We try hard at giving our children the lessons that will teach them how to be all they can be: music classes, multiple sports, summer camps, advanced classes and club memberships. We feel that we are being good parents because we are providing our children with all these structured activities.

However, the more we want for our children, the more structured and busy our lives become. We spend more time at work, drive longer for a higher paying job, volunteer for many organizations, attend PTA meetings and face other daily distractions. But unfortunately, we don't stop to think how little time we actually spend with our children. And most experts would agree that spending time with our children is much more important than any of the above activities.

When everyone does their own thing, they miss out on the comfort and support that family provides. Unfortunately, many American families have lost the ability to interact with each other. *Simple Principles to Raise a Successful Child* provides the road map back to a connected family life.

Who should read this book?

This book is for all parents who want their children to become happy, healthy, independent, confident and fulfilled. In other words, it's for *all* parents. The information contained in this book can be applied to children of all ages, from infants to teenagers. Parents practicing all kinds of parenting styles agree on the commonsense nature of the simple principles outlined herein.

This book also provides phrases to build self-esteem in children and questions parents can use to jump-start conversations with their children. These phrases and questions will help you gain the love and respect of your children.

This book is for parents who want to:
- feel closer to their children
- feel more in control
- reduce the amount of conflict in the house
- motivate their children to do better in school
- increase confidence about parenting
- lessen the amount of sibling rivalry in the household
- find specific activities to bond more with their children
- encourage spirituality and strong moral values in their children
- develop a united parenting strategy with their spouse

- encourage a more positive outlook or world view in their children
- focus their children on the more meaningful, non-material aspects of life

Even if your children are involved with drugs or troublesome friends, you'll find that implementing just a few of these principles will begin to turn their behavior around. This easy-to-read, inspirational book is sure to make a difference for parents who long to have a happier family life.

Why should you read this book?

It is clear that positive, involved relationships with parents are critical to children's success. Without these relationships, children suffer. It is clear that the lack of parental communication is strongly associated with feeling less happy. And the less happy children are, the more they turn to smoking, alcohol and bad behavior.

While parents thought that the acceptance letters to the best colleges, the entry-level jobs at the most respected companies, and the acquisition of bigger homes and cars would result in the happiest and most successful children, quite the opposite is true.

While our closets and garages are packed with material comforts, Americans are some of the loneliest people on the planet. The average American has only two close friends, and 25% have absolutely no one in whom to confide. Longer work hours, the tendency to relocate and our dependence on e-mail for connection is to blame for our lack of real connection with others.

Simple Principles to Raise a Successful Child provides a comprehensive list of the most crucial tenets parents need to raise children who are successful in every aspect of their lives. Accomplishment in careers, satisfaction in relationships, acceptance of self and the achievement of inner peace and happiness need not be left to chance. In these pages, you'll learn how to demonstrate love while setting limits, encouraging self-esteem, communicating effectively, motivating children to find their strengths and reacting appropriately when children cross boundaries. The principles are short and written simply so you can understand them quickly and put them into practice right away. These are the principles that create successful children.

The Challenges of Raising Children Today

Raising successful children isn't supposed to be difficult, especially considering all the gains made by generations before us. We are living in an age that provides the best standard of living, the most opportunities for the greatest number of people, the best medical care and the most exciting entertainment ever. The United States is one of the richest nations in the world. According to the National Association of Home Builders, the size of the typical new house more than doubled between the years 1950 and 2000, from 983 square feet to 2,434 square feet. Each day in America, close to sixty people become millionaires.

Despite the tremendous opportunities available in American society, many young people astound us with their lack of motivation, rudeness and disrespect of elders, each other and even themselves. Vast numbers of our youth lack direction, demonstrate a reluctance to take responsibility for their actions and seem unhappy and hopeless.

The rate of experimental and risky behavior is a further indication of the trouble our children face. At parent meetings in middle schools we hear horror stories about sex parties where children as young as 10 participate. A large percentage of U.S. high school students report heavy episodic drinking (five or more alcoholic drinks in a row) more often than we can imagine.

Suicide is the third leading cause of death for youth between the ages of 15 and 24 nationwide.

Where Did We Go Wrong?

If you're blaming yourself for your family's lack of harmony and your children's troubles, understand that forces beyond you have contributed to both. The unique history of this country has both benefited and undermined us. The motivation to personal success has raised the United States to the level of a superpower in both the economic and military arenas.

Yet these advantages have come at a price. The strong family traditions that came with immigrants from all over the world have been diluted by the desire for individual achievement. This shift took place most drastically in the past fifty years. While many of the changes success brings are positive, its effect on our children is often less than positive.

In the search for self-fulfillment and a better lifestyle, individuals have moved away from their mothers and fathers, aunts and uncles and grandparents to find jobs in other cities and states. We now exist mostly in small nuclear families with no extended family support. Driven by success, we work long hours to increase our standard of living and productivity, and to boost our company's profit margins. We have moved family, friendship and community to the margins of our lives.

It is time American society refocused on meaningful family connections. *Simple Principles to Raise a Successful Child* guides parents in finding what their children need for true satisfaction and success in life.

What Are We Missing?

The drive to succeed, coupled with participation in activities designed to enhance our personal skills, can be invigorating and hard to give up. But this adherence to self-actualization has failed the individual in dire ways.

First, our loss of connection to extended family has robbed us of much guidance as we raise our own children. Having older family members around benefits parents in many ways. They help reinforce our disciplinary style and oversee us as parents. They provide needed emotional support to energize us and give us confidence to act as parents to our children rather than their friends. Plus, having relatives in close proximity to babysit also gives parents a much needed break! Without them, parenting is more stressful.

Secondly, the lost time with our children has complicated family life. Most notably, it has created a sense of guilt that makes us reluctant to discipline our children. Without the time invested, we don't know our children as well as we could, making it tougher to tailor our discipline to their specific personalities. We don't have as many opportunities to impart our values. We often feel deserving of our children's disrespect and anger and don't stamp it out when it arises. This fallout from over-complicated lives can't help but lead to compromised bonds between parents and children.

What Do Our Children Need?

Faced with the challenges of this era, it is still possible to raise a successful child. What children need most from parents is simple: a firm foundation of love and consistent discipline that helps them learn to control their impulses and understand their own behavior. *Simple Principles to Raise a Successful Child* provides the time-tested principles that, when consistently practiced, will help ensure that your child becomes self-confident, respectful, emotionally stable and fulfilled.

Maximizing the Benefits of This Book

When you read this book, make sure to leave it out and refer to it often so that your discipline and strategies remain consistent. Because American parents are so busy, we tend to forget much of what we read, and we need information to be constantly reinforced. This book states each principle and then briefly explains its significance in a format that is very simple to read. When something happens with your children, come back to this book. It will serve as reassurance that you did the right thing or guide you to do better next time. It will also give you resources and direction to search in depth for more information on issues that seem to be prevalent in your household.

The principles are broken down into categories that address different aspects of your child's well-being. The most important chapter comes first: "Making Your Children Feel Loved." Next we include principles covering discipline, communication, self-esteem, education, outside influences, belonging, motivation and spirituality. These principles will give you specific strategies to help your child grow successfully in each of these areas. You will also find principles to help you become a good parent, teacher or caregiver. We even provide words to praise your children. The more you use these words, the more successful your children will become. Last, but not least, we include questions to ask your children and questions to ask yourself. These questions will allow you to maintain good communication with your children and will help you get to know them better.

After you finish reading this book, and often thereafter, think of something your child has done that you're concerned about. Turn to the appropriate section and browse the principle that best fits. At the back of the book, you'll find some phrases to use to begin discussing the subject with your children.

Making Your Children Feel Loved

Of course, no parent needs to be told that love makes all the difference in raising happy, successful children. It's more difficult, however, to understand how to best translate the tremendous love we have for our children into the words and actions that bolster them and strengthen our relationships. Some parents believe they are showing love by being very stern, critical and controlling. These parents have been labeled "authoritarian." They rule without listening to their children's explanation of the situation.

Because positive encouragement works far better than threats and punishments, there are many more incentives to love and be kind in this book than there are to be stern. Hugging your children regularly creates a physical bond that comforts, calms and enables them to listen. In a world where playground and school atmospheres are often tough, children cannot hear the words "I love you" enough.

Love, regularly expressed, works miracles. Experts have found that the presence of positive intimate relationships shortens healing time after an operation, increases the chances of heart attack survival, and reduces the odds of disease occurrence and recurrence. Children respond best to demonstrated love. They're more confident and inclined to excel in school when they know they're loved. Teenagers who feel worthy of love and respect are less likely to use drugs or become involved in unhealthy relationships.

Principle #1

Tell your children you love them
several times a day,
maybe more.

※

Because parents and children can conflict with each other throughout the day or week, it's important to temper these minor tensions with declarations of love. Assurances of a parent's love make children much less likely to engage in self-destructive behaviors. Children never get tired of hearing that you love them.

PRINCIPLE #2

Play the "Guess What?" game with your young children.

---　✳　---

Ask your children, "Guess what?" When they answer, "What?" Say, "Mommy/Daddy loves you!" Play this game often. Always give the same answer. After a while, when someone asks them "Guess what?" they will think, "Mommy/Daddy loves me." By playing this game, you set up a format to remind your children of your love wherever they may go. Many experts agree that a child's sense of how much he or she is loved is crucial to create healthy relationships of his or her own.

PRINCIPLE #3

Play with and tickle
your children often.

———————— ❊ ————————

Play physically with your young children and laugh with them. The physical acts of smiling and laughing release endorphins in the brain which create better moods that can last all day.

Principle #4

Be affectionate.

---- ✳ ----

Children feel loved when they are touched affectionately by a parent. A pat on the back, a warm smile, a high five and a wink take so little effort, yet mean so much to your children. People who are more affectionate report higher levels of happiness, self-esteem, social activity and mental health. They have less stress, depression, fear of intimacy and social isolation.

PRINCIPLE #5

Carry your children often, before they get too big.

———— ✳ ————

This closeness creates a special bond between you and your children. Babies who are carried more cry less. Instead, they are able to engage in a state of "quiet alertness" where they can best observe and learn from the world around them.

Principle #6

Enjoy the early years when
your children still want
to be close to you.

---- ✳ ----

Soon enough, the time will come when your children will not
want to spend every waking moment with you. Never will
anyone else be so enamored of you. Cherish it while you can!

PRINCIPLE #7

Make eye contact with your children, then smile and tell them you love them.

❋

Eye contact is crucial in the formation of loving bonds. When you cannot look someone in the eye, it indicates that your feelings for that person may be compromised or ambivalent. Eye contact also shows sincerity and assures your children that you are telling the truth.

PRINCIPLE #8

Learn the power of hugs.
Hug your children frequently.

Also hug your spouse, parents, in-laws and friends. Nearly everyone feels better after a hug because affection reduces the levels of cortisol, a stress hormone, in the brain. The more affection people receive, the less stress they feel.

PRINCIPLE #9

When you must reprimand bad behavior, follow up with messages of love.

———————— ✳ ————————

Once the situation has cooled down and some time has passed, try to say something positive to your children or be affectionate with them. Reassurances will convince your children that you do not think they are bad to the core and that you are not punishing them just to be mean.

Teaching Self-Discipline

The most necessary outgrowth of love is discipline. Discipline is the second most important thing a parent can give a child. Love is the first. The most important aspect of discipline is setting limits and following through with consequences when those limits are breached. This is the most difficult, stressful and aggravating aspect of parenting. Perhaps that's why parents are struggling with it.

According to many leading child welfare organizations, American parents these days are having a tough time setting and sticking to rules. With both parents working and children involved in so many after school activities, parents and children have less time for each other. When they are together, some parents are reluctant to use that precious time in a way they think is negative. Spending time scolding or imparting consequences is dismaying when there are only a few hours in the day to interact with your children.

While this reluctance is understandable, it harms our children. Some parents tend to become friends with their children, abnegating their authority. Lax discipline only creates children who are spoiled and at the same time, lacking in self-esteem. While they have almost everything they want with no standards to live up to, these middle-class children do not believe in their own abilities and character, a poverty far more dire and damaging than a lack of material goods.

We need a departure from consumer society and a return to a code of morality that emphasizes consistent discipline and time spent together. We seem to have a disconnection between being strict and loving our children. Setting a rule or limit will not impede the formation of close bonds with our children. Quite the contrary, study after study demonstrates that it reinforces the parent/child bond because children respect the parent for setting and sticking to boundaries. Further, children know deep down that the parent who disciplines does so with their best interests in mind.

We give in to our children because we haven't spent enough time with them. Parents consistently report that work obligations are the number one obstacle to being a better parent. Children sense this guilt and use it to their advantage. Parents who create rules and consistently enforce them have happier, more well-adjusted and eventually more successful children. *Simple Principles to Raise a Successful Child* provides all the guidance you'll need for disciplining with love.

Consider these statistics about high school students from the Centers for Disease Control:
- 54% have tried cigarettes
- 74% have tried at least one alcoholic drink
- 47% have had sexual intercourse

It's amazing that children are getting the opportunities to participate in these behaviors. Clearly, they're not as well supervised as children in previous generations. With parents second-guessing themselves, children feel they have unspoken permission to seek out situations where they can experiment. But we all know that premature involvement with these behaviors leads to failure in school.

This trend toward lax discipline and reduced involvement is getting the attention of America's leading child advocacy organizations. Both the American Academy of Pediatrics and the Child Welfare League of America caution parents that trying to be their children's friends only backfires. These organizations stress that close bonds with our children develop best when parents set strict limits and enforce them. Children will have scores of friends, but they only get two parents to teach them consistent discipline.

When you discipline your children sensibly, they will know you love them. Set rules around your house so that your children will know what is expected. Take time to explain why the rules are important. If rules are transgressed, be sure to give your child a consequence that fits the misbehavior. Once you set a rule, stick to it. Similarly, if you say no to a request, stick to it. Inconsistency will either confuse your children or encourage them to pester you until you give in.

That said, when children do cross boundaries, do not make them feel like they themselves are failures. Focus on the behavior and explain that the action is inconsistent with the good children that they are. Try to get all the information that led to the behavior before coming up with a consequence. In the end, children will appreciate that you're protecting them from their own unruly impulses and taking the time to understand how those impulses overwhelmed them in the first place.

Principle #10

Provide the discipline, consistency and
structure children need to feel
safe and happy.

※

Children need a structured home environment where there are
rules they can depend on to control their own behaviors. It has
been proven that children with consistent parents who enforce
rules are more likely to stay out of trouble later in life.

PRINCIPLE #11

When your children do something wrong, never tell them they are bad people.

---— ❋ ———

Rather, focus on the behavior. Remind them that they are good girls or boys and that good girls or boys don't do what they did. Even good children make poor choices sometimes. If your children see themselves as good, bad behaviors will only feel more wrong to them as they get older.

Principle #12

Don't forget to reward good behavior just as you would punish bad behavior.

---- ❊ ----

Positive feedback helps your children to excel. Whenever your children remember to follow the rules, praise and encourage them. You do not need any elaborate system of rewards; simply acknowledge the good behavior (e.g. "Thank you for bringing your plates to the sink") and give your children hugs.

PRINCIPLE #13

Be careful saying "no."
When you use it, you
must stick to it.

---------------------- ✳ ----------------------

Let your children know that "yes" means yes and "no" means no. If you say "no" and later change your mind, your children will think that if they insist or fuss long enough, you will change your mind. Young children will repeat a request an average of nine times before giving up. Teenagers have been known to ask for the same thing up to fifty times.

Principle #14

Teach your children the meaning of the word "nonnegotiable."

———————— ✳ ————————

When you absolutely don't want your children to do something, tell them it is "nonnegotiable," and then tell them why you feel they should not do it. Save this word for very serious issues. They should learn that when you say, "nonnegotiable," you will never change your mind.

Principle #15

Make the natural consequences of your children's choices clear to them.

✳

Instead of saying, "Sit down at that desk and do your homework because I say so," try, "If you don't get the homework done, you'll have to go to your teacher tomorrow and explain that you didn't get it done because you wanted to play." These consequences will be more powerful in getting your children to do what you want.

PRINCIPLE #16

Encourage and reward good behavior at school.

————————— ✳ —————————

While you may think your children are rewarded enough at school, you should reinforce their good work with acknowledgement at home too. An appropriate reward could be a trip to the movies or a book they've been eager to read. Let them know that good study habits will be important as they get older.

Principle #17

Be strict and don't let your children get away with bad behavior.

※

When you are strict, your children will know that you care enough to prevent them from making mistakes that could affect the rest of their lives. They also know that you are trying to help them become good people. The most successful parents are those who create rules and apply consequences when rules are broken.

PRINCIPLE #18

Allow children to learn how to correct their own mistakes.

❋

As a parent, your job is to offer guidance and suggestions, but giving your children the solutions to all their problems will prevent them from becoming fully independent.

PRINCIPLE #19

When your children ask, "Why not?"
be ready to explain your reasons
for saying "no."

※

Children deserve truthful answers from their parents. When you don't explain your reasons, they might not believe that your opinion is valid. Explaining your reasoning also shows your children that you place restrictions on their activities for their own benefit. Explaining your reasons will also help you dodge the term "controlling" when your children are in their teenage years.

Principle #20

When your children raise their voices
or speak disrespectfully, don't be
tempted to answer in
the same tone.

Simply say, "Excuse me! What tone of voice is that? Where did that come from? Where did you learn to speak that way?" They may have just lost control momentarily. Give your children a chance to think about why they were speaking so disrespectfully, and they may avoid those circumstances in the future.

Principle #21

When you have to say "no," but
can't come up with a good reason,
simply say, "I cannot let you do
that because I love you."

---- ❋ ----

This will give you some time to think. You can also buy time
by telling your children that you will discuss it further later.
Give yourself a chance to get your thoughts together. Otherwise, your reasoning may not be so convincing.

Principle #22

Be consistent when applying consequences.

--- ✳ ---

Don't set a rule, limit, consequence or even a reward unless you are going to be consistent in enforcing it. Inconsistent discipline teaches your children to manipulate you and press your emotional buttons.

Principle #23

When your children do something
wrong and you fear you may lose
your temper, say, "What kind of
behavior is that?" and send
the children to their rooms.

———————————— ✳ ————————————

This move gives you and your children time to think afterwards. Sending your children to their rooms after misbehavior will prevent you from saying or doing something that you will later regret.

Principle #24

When your children are doing something dangerous, use a message of love such as, "It will hurt me tremendously if anyone gets hurt, so please stop doing that!"

❋

Focusing on the dangerous situation lets your children know that you are not angry at them. If you speak harshly during a dangerous situation like, "Stop! A car is coming!" or "Hot! The pan is hot!" Follow up with a hug so that you can reconnect.

PRINCIPLE #25

When your children want to do something you disapprove of, ask them what someone they respect would think of their behavior.

✳

For instance, "What would Michael Jordan (U.S. basketball star) think of you watching television all day?" or, "Would Tiger Woods (famous golfer) put a stud through his tongue?" Children sometimes assert themselves by making decisions that shock or anger their parents. When this happens, parents can call upon the image of respected adults outside of the family to make a point to their children.

Principle #26

Whenever there is a conflict between you and your children, ask them what they would do if they were the parent.

---- ❋ ----

Ask your children the following questions: "How do you think we should handle this?" "What would you do in my situation?" "What do you propose we do?" Asking these and other questions will provide your children with a sense of responsibility for the situation and will empower them to make the right decision.

PRINCIPLE #27

If you yell at your children when they
are young, your children will yell
at you when you are old.

❋

If you have a loud household where you're often raising your
voice, your children will view this environment as normal.
They will replicate it as adults. When you feel you're going to
lose it, do your best to leave the situation by taking a time-out
for yourself.

Principle #28

Don't let your children tell lies. Punish a child for any lie, no matter how insignificant.

---　✳　---

Teach your children that trust between parents and children is the most important part of maintaining a good, solid relationship. Make sure they realize that trust between two people takes time and effort to establish and can be lost with one little lie. Once lost, it can take years to earn that trust back.

Principle #29

Before you punish your children for misbehavior, determine what caused it.

---- ❊ ----

You may discover legitimate reasons for your children's behavior. While the behavior might be inappropriate, discuss why they acted that way and help them find better ways to respond to such problems in the future. Then, set the punishment based on what they did and why they did it.

PRINCIPLE #30

Remember that you have influence over your children's behavior, not control.

✳

Children in authoritarian families where one or both parents have absolute control do not always know how to behave when outside the family. It is better to give your children enough freedom to choose the right path on their own, as this will help them gain confidence in their own decision-making skills.

Principle #31

Do reward your child.
Do not bribe your child.
Know the difference.

---- ✳ ----

A reward is received after a good behavior is carried out. A bribe is a promise given in advance of a specific behavior. If you bribe your children, they will resist performing a good act without the promise of a reward. It is best to let children focus on the good feelings surrounding their positive behavior. Those will soon become reward enough to encourage good behavior in the future.

Principle #32

Help your children learn how
to make the best choices
for themselves.

※

Children must learn that life is filled with choices. You can help
your children develop decision-making skills by giving them
the opportunity to make choices from the time they are very
young. Even simple decisions, such as whether to read a book
or watch television, provide a valuable learning opportunity.

Principle #33

Take time to set household rules and to explain the reasons behind them.

※

Consider asking your children to help you create the rules for certain behavior. Children involved in setting rules respect them more. Post rules in an obvious place to remind your children of them daily.

Principle #34

Explain to your children that their
misbehavior at home will be
far less tolerated outside
the family.

When you discipline your children, you are teaching them
how to make their way in society. Tell them that the behaviors
you won't put up with won't be tolerated by teachers, friends,
bosses and co-workers either. Good discipline is about teaching what the world will tolerate and what it won't.

Principle #35

Always discipline with an eye to shaping behavior. Do not discipline to satisfy a desire to hurt or get revenge.

❉

If you are so angry that you find pleasure in punishing your children, it may be necessary to find some guidance of your own. Your actions can be detrimental to the development of your children.

Principle #36

Pay attention to your children's reaction to your limits and consequences.

✳

If your child is extremely angry about limits you have set, maybe your limits are too stringent, or perhaps you may not have made the reason for the limit clear enough. It is okay to reassess your limits and adjust them occasionally.

Principle #37

Do not assume your children
understand what they
did was wrong.

✳

You must explain why their actions were wrong. Make sure
that your explanation fits with both your children's stage of
development and their temperament.

PRINCIPLE #38

Choose your battles wisely.

---- ❈ ----

There will be many situations where you and your children do not see eye to eye. Don't sweat the small stuff. As long as no one is getting harmed, try to keep the household atmosphere as positive as possible by ignoring minor or silly misbehaviors.

Principle #39

When trying to change or shape your children's behavior, set your sites on reasonable and attainable goals.

———————————— ✳ ————————————

With your children's help, brainstorm some intermediate steps to tailor their behavior. That way, you can both feel relieved and rewarded when each intermediate step is achieved.

Maintaining Good Communication

Since most of us aren't child development experts, we may not fully understand our children's unique way of translating the world. While we think we're speaking clearly, children may interpret our words and body language in ways very differently from what we intend. By using the communication principles discussed in this chapter, you'll discover the most effective strategies you can use to talk with children whose minds are still developing.

Communication works best when both sides trust that they're being heard. To show your children you're interested in their thoughts and ideas, ask them their opinions about what's going on at school, at home or in the world. Repeat their response and show your approval. When your children come to you with a problem, often they just want to talk and express how they're feeling without advice from you. If you hold off on suggestions and give them a chance to come up with their own solutions, they will appreciate you all the more.

You will further demonstrate respect for your children and their intelligence when you listen to what they are saying and show that you value their decisions. Children whose decisions are valued by their parents are better able to resist peer pressure and other harmful influences from the media and the outside world. Children need to know that communication goes both ways, and that they are not simply on the receiving end of a stream of strict orders.

If you feel your children don't discuss what is going on in their lives enough and your relationship is suffering for it, turn to the "Questions to Ask" section, starting on page 257. There you will find all kinds of questions that will elicit specific answers on topics children want to talk to their parents about. You will find questions that will fit your situation. With these examples to get you started, you can create and tailor your own style of communicating with your children. Don't be surprised to find that each of your children requires a different approach.

Principle #40

If you are having problems
communicating with your
children, find a positive
role model to help.

※

This person should be someone your children admire and respect. Every parent turns elsewhere for support sometimes.
Do not feel like a failure. At least you're savvy enough to
know you cannot handle the situation alone.

Principle #41

Teach your children the art of conversation.

———————— ❊ ————————

Tell your children that if they ask others questions about themselves, they will be regarded as smart, freethinking and fun. Help your children develop a few icebreaker lines to get conversations started.

Principle #42

If you have two children and you tell one child that he or she is smart, tell the other one that he or she is smart, too.

✳

Giving too much attention to one child not only damages the other sibling's self-esteem but can also lead to sibling rivalry and bad feelings that may last for many years. Some researchers believe that 75% of individual personality differences are attributed to how the family treated a particular sibling.

Principle #43

Be conscious of whether you're favoring a child for having more of your traits than your other children.

---- ⁕ ----

Parents sometimes view one child as having more positive character traits than others when it could simply be that one child resembles that parent more. Conversely, when a parent has traits he or she regrets, the parent may take his or her frustrations out on the child with similar traits. Be aware of just how you identify with your children.

PRINCIPLE #44

Talk to your children 10 to 15 minutes before they go to bed at night.

---※---

Each night, ask your children if they have any questions they'd like to ask you or ask them the questions listed in the back of this book. These questions are a fantastic opportunity for you to get to know your children better and spend quality time together.

PRINCIPLE #45

When trying to get information about their day, share something that happened to you.

❋

Parents often grill their children about what happened at school. Instead, try to think of things that happened to you throughout your day that you can share with your children. Sharing your personal events can help get the conversation started. They are just as interested about you as you are about them.

Principle #46

Teach your children to ask for what they want.

---　✳　---

While they may not always get it, they will have a much better chance of getting what they want if they simply ask. This will be an important lesson as they grow up.

PRINCIPLE #47

Monitor how many times you say "no" in a day. Try to find another way to discourage a child's behavior.

———————— ✳ ————————

The average American child hears the word, "no" or "don't" over 100,000 times while growing up. Unfortunately, children hear the word "yes" only a few thousand times. If your children hear "no" every time they ask a question, they will stop asking questions. Find out ways to turn "no" answers into "yes" ones. For example, if your children ask to play outside, do not say, "No, you need to finish your homework first." Instead reply, "Yes, as soon as you finish your homework."

Principle #48

Ask your children for their opinion about
everything and listen closely.

———————————————— ✳ ————————————————

When they answer, acknowledge their response and say
something to indicate that you really heard them. Doing this
will help your children develop their critical-thinking skills
and build their self-esteem.

PRINCIPLE #49

Try to establish a time in the day when your children know you are open to listening to them.

---- ❋ ----

In the morning during breakfast or at bedtime there are opportune moments to make yourself available to your children on a daily basis. Your children will look forward to that time so they can share with you whatever is bothering them.

PRINCIPLE #50

Don't concentrate on the negative.

❋

For example:
"I don't need your help."
"I don't have the time."
"We can't wait all day."
"Don't touch that."
"Don't say that."
"Don't be lazy."
"Don't do that."
"Don't move."
"Keep quiet."
"No!"

PRINCIPLE #51

Concentrate on the positive.

For example:

"Keep trying. You are doing very well."

"I can always count on you."

"You are so responsible."

"I love being with you."

"You make me happy."

"You make me proud."

"You are a great kid."

"You are so brave."

"You are so smart."

"You are gifted."

PRINCIPLE #52

Avoid negative phrases.

—— ❊ ——

For example:
"You're always getting in trouble."
"Hurry up! I can't wait all day."
"You are irresponsible."
"Where is your head?"
"You're in my way."
"You are a bad kid."
"Don't be so shy."

Principle #53

Use positive phrases.

✳

For example:
"I can't believe you did that all by yourself."
"It makes me proud to see you try."
"Your smile lights up this house."
"You are doing great!"
"Never say you can't."
"I like your ideas."
"Good job!"

PRINCIPLE #54

Avoid asking negative questions.

───────────── ✳ ─────────────

For example:
"How could you say such a thing?"
"How can you possibly do that?"
"Who taught you how to dress?"
"What is wrong with you?"
"Why are you so slow?"

Principle #55

Ask positive questions.

— ✳ —

For example:
"Did you do that all by yourself?"
"How did you do that so quickly?"
"How did you figure that out?"
"What makes you so smart?"
"Would you like to try it?"

PRINCIPLE #56

When you are angry, stop to think
about what you are going to
say before you say it.

---- ❊ ----

Try to avoid speaking to your children when you're overwhelmed with stress or anger. When you're frustrated, it's
sometimes easy to make harsh, even cruel statements. You
may not really mean them, but your children may never forget your words.

Principle #57

If you want your children to do something again, compliment the way they do it the first time.

✳

When you criticize the way your children approach a task, they will be reluctant and resentful when they have to do it again. Always remember that your children are neither perfect nor are they clones of you. They might not approach tasks the way that you do but that does not mean that their efforts are any less legitimate.

Principle #58

Don't expect perfection from a child or even a teenager.

--- ✳ ---

It's unrealistic to expect a young child or even a teenager to think or act like you would in any situation. They haven't gone through what you have gone through and they don't have your experience.

Principle #59

Treat every question your children ask seriously.

———————————— ❊ ————————————

When your children ask you a question that you consider silly, remember that question may be very important to them.

Principle #60

Remember, children do not develop positive or negative behaviors unless we reinforce one or the other.

---- ❋ ----

Children come to believe they are what they've been told they are. If you want your children to be good at sports, tell them frequently how proud you are of their skills, even if they aren't very good. Eventually they will come to believe in themselves which is the first step to succeeding in anything.

Principle #61

If your children don't answer when you ask them a personal question, keep asking.

✳

Show your children that you are really interested in them and they will answer. Children, especially as they get older, can become uncomfortable sharing their private thoughts with their parents. Be patient and show that you care about them and want to know what is going on in their life, and they will open up to you.

PRINCIPLE #62

Teach your children the art of listening and understanding someone else's point of view.

---- ✳ ----

Listening to others and understanding multiple points of view is a valuable skill for good decision making. Impress upon your children that much can be learned from others. Teach them to value the minds and experiences of people from backgrounds different from their own.

Principle #63

Try to keep quiet when your children are sharing a problem with you.

---※---

Often when children share something that happened to them, they are not looking for an opinion, lecture or advice. They just want to be heard. Children respond well to *active listening*, when you paraphrase what they have said and then say it back to them. Once children hear their problems expressed, they're better able to process and solve them on their own.

PRINCIPLE #64

Tell your children that it really makes you happy when they say they love you or when they ask you to hold them or spend time with them.

※

They will do these things more often when they know how much you enjoy their affection. Why should your children tell you that they love you if they don't know that it's important to you? Children want to do all they can to make their parents happy.

PRINCIPLE #65

Put an end to subtle put-downs, sarcasm and criticism.

———————— ❋ ————————

If you find yourself directing these behaviors toward your children, stop immediately. You will not accomplish anything with this and will greatly jeopardize the relationship with your children.

Principle #66

Children have radar. Though you may think that they are in their own little world, they are always listening to every word you say.

---　*　---

Because of this, you should always think before you speak, and make sure that what you say around your children is positive, helpful and kind.

Principle #67

When children ask you how to handle a particular situation, ask them how they think they should handle it first.

---------------------- ❋ ----------------------

One of the most important things your children must learn is how to think for themselves. If you give them the opportunity, they will learn how to navigate life's moral quandaries through trial and error and eventually come to trust their own judgment.

PRINCIPLE #68

Be cautious of your tone and body
language when you speak
to your children.

---- ❋ ----

Often, it is not what you say to your children that matters,
but the way in which you say it. Negative body language and
tone can subvert your praise and sincerity. Be alert! Send clear
signals to your children and make sure your tone and body
language reinforce your message, not undermine it.

Principle #69

Ask your children their opinions on major family decisions.

By asking their opinions on the prospect of going to a new school, moving to a new house or having a relative stay over, you show them that their feelings always count. If they feel their input is valued, children will be happier about the final decision, even if their choice isn't ultimately accepted.

PRINCIPLE #70

When encouraging and complimenting
your children, focus on efforts
rather than results.

❄

It is impressive when the shy child gets out there on the soc-
cer field or when the overweight child turns down the milk
shake. The points scored and the weight lost will come after
the efforts are made. These attempts require great fortitude
and willpower and should be praised.

PRINCIPLE #71

When you give your children consequences for misbehavior, remember to explain what they did wrong.

❋

Children cannot learn from misbehavior if they do not understand what they did wrong. Young children, especially those under the age of eight, do not always know the difference between right and wrong. It should be explained to them in clear, straightforward terms.

PRINCIPLE #72

Set a good example for your children.

––––––––––––––––––––––––– ❊ –––––––––––––––––––––––––

Parents are children's first and most influential role models. If you don't set a good example, your children will inherit your bad behavior. If you don't listen to them, they will not want to listen to you.

Principle #73

Eliminate the following words
from your vocabulary:
Always
Never

✳

These are absolutes that don't really occur in interpersonal situations. Children will only find the use of these terms unfair.

PRINCIPLE #74

Create a habit of a dialogue, not a monologue.

✳

When speaking to your children make sure you're not doing all the talking. Avoid preaching. Make sure there is a back and forth sharing of ideas and opinions. Listen to them and respect their views and ideas.

Developing Self-Esteem

Even when parents are careful to communicate effectively and demonstrate their love in a warm, positive way, it can still be tricky to foster confidence in our children. Unlike what the psychologists of the 1970s' self-esteem movement believed, children cannot absorb confidence simply through parents' kind words and encouragement. Words fall short when the results of our children's efforts don't back up the praise lavished upon them. Children need to have concrete proof that what they've done is worthy of such praise.

Self-esteem flourishes when children are given the freedom and opportunity to master tasks. Exposure to mastery can start at the youngest ages. Letting preschoolers choose the fresh fruit at the supermarket gives them a sense of accomplishment. Older children need the freedom to explore their interests. Becoming involved in sports and school activities allows children to see just where their talents lie. When they succeed, they add another aspect to their identity. If they are not so successful, they are free to move on to the next challenge where they may excel. Chores around the house give children and teenagers a sense of meaning as they contribute to the smooth operation of the household. Once they view themselves as reliable and hardworking, their confidence increases.

As parents, we mirror our children to themselves. We show our children just who they really are by giving them feedback. If you honor, respect and even praise your children's feelings, thoughts and ideas, they will internalize that they are important members of society. Fostering self-confidence isn't as easy as it may first appear.

With the principles listed here, parents can fill their children with the knowledge that they are valuable individuals whom society will come to depend upon in the years ahead.

Principle #75

Compliment! Compliment! Compliment!

※

This is one of the most basic principles for creating successful children. It builds self-esteem and confidence. Phrases like, "You got into the shower without whining!" "You ate all your carrots! Wow!" or "You're such a fast dresser!" reward children and tell them that they did the right thing. When they know their efforts are recognized, children are happy to repeat them.

PRINCIPLE #76

Tell your children they make you proud.

--- ✳ ---

Children need to hear your approval. Praise from parents lets your children know that they fit well into the family. A child with a strong sense of belonging is more likely to follow the family's rules. Teenagers who have a close connection with caring and approving parents are less likely to drink, smoke and behave promiscuously.

PRINCIPLE #77

Teach your children the benefits of exercise.

※

Exercise makes children strong, not only physically, but also emotionally. Children involved in physical fitness feel healthier, have more confidence, and make friends more easily than those who do not exercise.

Principle #78

Expose your children to theater and the arts.

---　✳　---

Art and theater help bring important ideas to life. They help us understand what it is to be human. Most communities have local theaters that perform plays geared toward children. If your own child is creative, early exposure to the arts may help him or her find direction sooner.

Principle #79

Let your children resolve their own conflicts with others.

❋

Act as a coach to guide your children through conflict resolution, but let them confront the offending party by themselves. Children need opportunities to realize that they can handle these situations by themselves.

PRINCIPLE #80

Teach your children that their worst enemy is fear of failing.

---　❋　---

It's important for our children to believe that it's okay to fail as long as they try their best. If they don't try, the only sure outcome is failure.

Principle #81

Encourage your children to complete homework, household and other tasks by themselves, even if you could do it quicker.

Children discover their skills by testing them out. Let your young children make their own beds. Older children can set the table or unload the dishwasher. These activities foster your children's independence and self-worth. They also demonstrate that you have confidence in your children's ability to handle problems and accomplish tasks.

Principle #82

When your young children accomplish something difficult or do something well, make a big deal out of it.

---　❋　---

Tell them you can't believe a child that age could do that! Tell your children often how proud you are of them. Complimenting your children lets them know that you believe they are capable of doing fantastic things. This encouragement gives them the confidence to accomplish even more.

PRINCIPLE #83

Give household duties to your children even from a very early age.

✳

Responsibilities make your children feel valuable and needed in the family, thus increasing their self-esteem. Children acquire useful skills when they start carrying out tasks early. Call a task "special" and it's more likely to get done.

Principle #84

Teach your children to use polite phrases.

---- ❊ ----

Use phrases such as: "Could you please…" "Thank you…" "Excuse me…" "Yes, please…" and "May I…" Good manners will make your children welcome wherever they go. The more positively society regards your children, the better they will feel about themselves. Using good manners also shows children that if they treat people with respect, they will be respected in turn.

Principle #85

Teach your children to look people in the eyes when they talk to them.

※

Explain that when people don't make eye contact, they are often perceived as dishonest. Make sure you make eye contact with your children as well.

PRINCIPLE #86

Remember important events that your children will be involved with on a particular day.

---·❋·---

Say things like, "Good luck on your test today!" or, "Remember to make eye contact when you're giving your presentation," or, "Drink plenty of water at your practice today; it's very hot!" Statements like these let children know you are aware of what's going on in their lives. You can even leave messages in the form of notes on the refrigerator or in your children's lunch boxes. When you take the time to acknowledge your children's activities, they will feel you are genuinely connected to them.

Principle #87

Get your children involved in team sports.

Children who participate in organized team sports learn to socialize, make friends and deal with personal conflicts. All these skills are valuable lessons for when they grow up.

PRINCIPLE #88

Find extracurricular activities for your children that are not sports-related.

※

There are many avenues to success in school and beyond. Some children are more suited for involvement in music, artistic or intellectual pursuits. The most important thing is to give your children an opportunity to excel in an area outside of school. Activities also give children larger groups from which to derive a sense of belonging.

Principle #89

Honor and validate your children's feelings and points of view.

✳

Even if you are making the final decision on a subject, take your children's thoughts into consideration and let them know their opinions are important. When you consider your children's input, they will know you value their ideas and appreciate their character. This recognition will make them feel worthwhile.

Principle #90

Find specific things to praise in your children's work or play.

—— ❈ ——

Using phrases like, "You played a great defensive game!" or, "I like all those colors you used!" are more likely to convince your children that you're paying attention and are sincerely impressed with what they've done. Even when the overall performance isn't spectacular, you can always find something to praise.

Principle #91

When your children ask you for help in doing something, ask them to try it again before stepping in.

✳

If they are still unable to do it, show them what they are doing wrong and let them try it again. If they still fail, help them to do it, but make sure they can either do part of it or at least learn by watching you do it. Tell them that you think they will be able to do it themselves next time.

Principle #92

If your children seem to have low
self-esteem, do whatever it
takes to raise it.

✳

Read books, spend time one-on-one with your child or consider counseling. Children with low self-esteem hang out with underachievers, do not excel in school and have a harder time resisting drugs and other temptations. It is critical to build your child's self-esteem from the time they are young.

Principle #93

Make sure you're not in the habit of continually pointing out what your children are doing wrong.

❋

If you constantly tell your children how misguided their actions are, they will become too discouraged to try anything new. If they know only what they do wrong and not what they do right, children can't create clear goals for proper behavior or strategies in their minds. Children need a concrete model of correct behavior in order to work toward it.

Principle #94

Say positive things about your children to others and make sure your children hear you.

———————— ✳ ————————

This makes them feel wonderful because they know you're not saying it to manipulate them in any way. Doing so can be even more powerful than directly telling them what you think of them.

PRINCIPLE #95

Never say anything negative about your children in front of them.

❋

Your approval and disapproval is more important than anything else to your children. Remember this point when talking to or about your children. If in conversation you tell your friend that your child does not like to get up in the morning, you are reinforcing that behavior in your child. Discussing your child's weaknesses can also lead to having them exhibit the negative behavior more often.

PRINCIPLE #96

Never compare your children with other people in a negative way.

※

For example, never say things like, "You will never be like your mother" "You are much slower than he is" or, "Your brother never did that." You should not expect your children to be identical to one another or to their parents or their friends. Each child comes with his or her own mixed bag of strengths and weaknesses. Comparisons only lead children to ignore their own strengths.

Principle #97

Treat your children with respect and dignity.

--- ✳ ---

Just because your children are young does not mean that they do not deserve respect. Teach them that everyone is entitled to being treated decently, no matter what their age, race or status. Always model how to treat individuals respectfully, starting with your own children.

Principle #98

Teach your children how to identify their emotions.

---　✳　---

It is important for children to be able to understand their feelings in order to be able to deal with them.

Principle #99

Teach your children how to express their feelings.

---- ✳ ----

While children should be free to air their feelings, they should not be permitted to hurt others physically or emotionally.

Principle #100

Help your children solve their
behavioral problems on their own.

❋

Ask your children what they think should be done about
their behavioral issues. Children's ideas and feelings are
worth listening to, as they might provide new solutions and
points of view. While children do not have the same amount
of experience as an adult, their perspectives can be helpful.

PRINCIPLE #101

Ask your children to teach you how to do something that they can do.

——————————— ✳ ———————————

Watch your children's faces light up when you make this request. Realizing that their parents don't know everything
gives children a little sense of power. Your appreciation of
their skills will enhance their self-esteem.

PRINCIPLE #102

Teach your children healthy eating habits at a young age.

❋

Proper nutrition ensures that your children will have the strength, energy and confidence they need to get through each day. A well balanced diet will help your children maintain a healthy weight and will also provide your children with the nutrients, vitamins and minerals necessary for them to become healthy adults. Also, individuals who learn good eating habits when they are young are more likely to retain them throughout adulthood.

PRINCIPLE #103

Teach your children proper personal hygiene.

———————— ❋ ————————

Cleanliness does not come naturally to children. Impress upon your children that teachers and other students will notice dirty cheeks or stains on their clothing. Children will feel better about themselves if they're not receiving snide comments from others.

PRINCIPLE #104

Show respect to your children.

---- ❋ ----

Recognize and acknowledge their physical and personal space, temperament, thoughts, opinions, feelings, privacy, beliefs.

PRINCIPLE #105

When your children ask you how to do or fix something, teach them the skills involved.

✳

Show your children how to pump up the bicycle tire, how to work the DVD player, search for information on the Internet or prepare their own cereal. The more skills children master, the more confidence they will have in their ability to conquer new, unfamiliar tasks.

PRINCIPLE #106

Teach your children to respect and protect their bodies.

❋

Use books, the Internet and educational television shows to show children how miraculous and fragile the human body is. With these images in mind, they will be more likely to take care of their bodies.

HELPING YOUR CHILDREN
BECOME GOOD STUDENTS

Some people think that the best predictors of success on the SAT is not a child's grades, school nor the amount of time spent on homework, but whether the family eats dinner together regularly. When children have the secure feelings that come from growing up in a loving and supportive household, they can absorb information without distraction. In this environment children can revel in the excitement that new knowledge brings.

Parents shape their children's perception of education. When parents model their belief that learning is one of life's greatest gifts, children will search for and succeed in the field to which they are most suited. Therefore, the first step is to let your children know how important it is that they do well in school. Studies show that the more education a person has, the higher salary he or she will receive.

School can be tricky for children. Use the principles in this section to help make your children's time in school as productive and enjoyable as possible.

Principle #107

Read often to your young children.

———————— ❋ ————————

Reading aloud to your children not only increases your emotional bonds but also encourages your children to want to read on their own.

Principle #108

Encourage reading.

---- ✳ ----

Reading stimulates the mind, fosters creativity, opens new worlds and provides fascinating facts to your children. The faster and better your children can read, the more their lives will be enriched.

PRINCIPLE #109

Find creative ways to read with your children.

---　✳　---

Set aside a night where you light candles and read mysteries or spooky stories to them. Have a regular night where you all sit around the living room reading silently to yourselves. Find a book that everyone likes and take turns reading from it out loud.

Principle #110

Read a story to your children and ask them questions about it.

---※---

For example, ask questions such as: "What would you have done if you were…?" "What did you like most about the story?" "What did you learn from the story?" and "What did you like the least?" Asking these questions will strengthen your child's ability to think critically. This also provides a great opportunity for you and your children to exchange ideas. Children will be glad you're asking for their opinions.

PRINCIPLE #111

Become involved in several different aspects of your children's school life.

———————— ✳ ————————

Children with parents involved in their school are more likely to succeed academically. Take your children to school. Meet their teachers and talk to them. Learn who their friends are and invite them over. Help out with or lead your children's extracurricular activities.

Principle #112

Teach your children how to use a computer from an early age.

---- ❋ ----

If computers are introduced as a fun learning tool, children will take all the benefits technology offers in stride. Without a computer, your child will be at a serious academic disadvantage later.

Principle #113

Find out if your children's school has an anti-bullying policy. If it doesn't, lead the fight to establish one.

※

School bullies can ruin the self-esteem of children who initially had a secure self-image. Don't let all your hard work be ruined by a disturbed child who bullies others. Encourage your children to share bullying incidents with you as they occur. Give your children the phrases and skills they need to discourage a bully's attention.

PRINCIPLE #114

Be selective when buying gifts.

---- ❋ ----

A large percentage of the gifts you buy your children should be educational toys. If your children don't have meaningless or violent toys at home, they will not miss them.

Principle #115

Encourage your children to learn a musical instrument or join a choir.

Learning how to sing or play an instrument is a skill that your children can enjoy for the rest of their lives. Listening to and playing music enhances cognitive functioning. It supports reasoning and math skills. Playing a musical instrument gives your children an area in which to test their skills and excel outside of school.

PRINCIPLE #116

Teach your children that strength
is gained by forming unions
with others.

Children need to learn that teamwork is the secret to success in many aspects of life. Impress upon them that another's strengths can support their own weak areas to create the best outcome.

PRINCIPLE #117

Teach through discovery.

———————————— ✳ ————————————

Become excited and surprised when your children bring you that big and scary spider. Use this opportunity to look up spiders on the Internet. Ask your children if they would like to be a spider. Remember, there are no wrong answers!

Principle #118

Teach children the value of money, saving and investing.

───────────── ❋ ─────────────

If you give your children allowances or if they receive money for their birthdays or holidays, suggest that they put some of the money in a savings account to buy something that they really want later on. Watching their money grow will be a great learning experience in investing. Also, encourage them to donate a small portion to those who have less.

PRINCIPLE #119

Teach your children how to speak in public from a very young age.

---※---

Competent public speaking is the key to success in any career. If you start early to desensitize your children to speaking in front of crowds, they will find this process as natural as brushing their teeth in the morning. This confidence will give them a great advantage in school and throughout their lives.

Principle #120

When your children are teenagers, have them read *Think and Grow Rich* by Napoleon Hill.

This best-selling book is a master motivator for anybody to be the best they can be. The main message of the book focuses on the idea that you can accomplish anything, if you have a desire to accomplish it and a burning strong belief that you can do it. Buy it for your children's bookshelf and encourage them to read through it from time to time.

Principle #121

Make sure your children eat a good,
well-balanced breakfast
each morning.

※

This habit is very important for success in school. Students who eat breakfast perform better in school than those who do not. They also report fewer feelings of anxiety and depression overall.

PRINCIPLE #122

Frame your children's report cards and put them on a wall in their bedroom.

---- ✳ ----

Seeing their achievement or lack thereof will motivate them to do the best they can in school. A's will look a lot better on their wall than C's.

PRINCIPLE #123

Teach your children to be respectful.

⁓

Children should know better than to damage their own or another's property, hurt others physically or emotionally and name call or use bad language. Many students exhibit these behaviors without regret. Make it clear to your children that this kind of disrespectful and hurtful behavior is unacceptable and is against your family's values. If your children are respectful they will become friends with respectful people and be less likely to fall into a bad crowd.

PRINCIPLE #124

Always ask your children questions that cannot be answered with a simple "yes" or "no" response.

---- ❋ ----

By asking more complex questions, you will be helping your children develop their own reasoning skills. A good time to try this is while you're driving in the car or when everyone is relaxed and there are no distractions.

Principle #125

Encourage your children to ask questions in school, at church, during lessons, etc.

Teach your children that the only stupid questions are the ones that don't get asked. Make it clear to them that if they are confused, it's likely others are as well.

Principle #126

Encourage your children to go
to bed at a reasonable hour.

Rested children can cope with the challenges of life much
better than tired ones.

PRINCIPLE #127

Make sure your young children have time to participate in unstructured play.

✳

When children get to create their own games, explore the backyard or spend time pretending, they are actually developing the critical and creative thinking skills they will need for higher levels of math and science. They will also feel happier and more peaceful.

Monitoring Outside
Influences

Parents may feel overwhelmed by the messages television and peers constantly give their children. Take comfort in the simple fact that parents have the most influence over their children's decisions, as long as they step up as respectable role models. We can limit outside influences by discussing with our children the motives behind others' attempts to influence them.

Parents can show children how deceptive advertising is, how television tries to make viewers believe they'll have more love, money or beauty if they only buy their product. Television shows are even worse. We need to take the opportunity to instruct our children how canned sitcoms and dramas depict an exaggerated and unrealistic world where no one lives. The producers pay their writers a lot of money to come up with fascinating, exciting scenarios. Our children cannot possibly compare their lives to those found on television.

Friends can make our lives rich and meaningful. Yet a bad friend can lead our children into behaviors that may haunt them all their lives. Explain to your children that friends don't necessarily have their best interest in mind. Friends often want to do things just for fun, to show off to others, or to build up their own self-esteem at the expense of your children's. Convince your children not to be drawn into situations that stem from a friend's unhealthy needs.

If you take the time to carefully explain your reasoning to your children (and if you have been fair in the past), your children will keep you as the central influential figure in their lives. Sure, they'll pitch a fit or two, but they need you to maintain limits and good role modeling so they can better understand how to behave themselves. Deep down, your children know this.

PRINCIPLE #128

Monitor what your children watch on television. What they see does affect their behavior.

— ❋ —

There is a strong link between exposure to violent TV and aggressive behavior in children and teenagers. Watching violence on television can lead to hostility, fear, anxiety, depression, nightmares, sleep disturbances and post-traumatic stress disorder.

PRINCIPLE #129

Limit the amount of television your children watch.

———————— ❋ ————————

Encourage your children to play with educational toys, read books or engage in imaginative games. These alternatives stimulate the brain far more than television or videos. Watching too much television exposes children to commercials for products they do not need. On average, children in the United States watch about four hours of TV every day.

PRINCIPLE #130

Keep the television off during dinner and other family time.

---------- ✳ ----------

Family meals are a great time to discuss the day's events that are either exciting or troubling for your children. You can also discuss anything that made them happy or proud of themselves. Use this opportunity to share events that occurred in your day as well. Teenagers who eat meals with their families on a regular basis have much lower incidence of cigarette, alcohol and substance abuse problems, depressive symptoms and suicidal thoughts. They also tend to do better at school.

Principle #131

Restrict your children from watching television at night.

Nighttime television is filled with violence, sex and other activities inappropriate for children. Instead, encourage your children to read, host a family game night or take a walk outside together and enjoy the fresh evening air. Explore the many entertainment alternatives to television.

PRINCIPLE #132

Know who your children's friends are.

---- ❋ ----

Encourage involvement with good friends, and strongly oppose involvement with bad friends. Friends influence your children's development in many ways. They can enhance or diminish feelings of self-esteem and happiness. One bad friend can ruin ten years of good parenting.

PRINCIPLE #133

Encourage your children's friends to hang out at your house.

※

When your children are older, invite their friends over and then give them limited privacy. Have lots of snacks, a ping pong table and other fun things available for them to do. Give them a reason to hang out at your house rather than at the mall or at someone else's home.

Principle #134

Teach your children that it is much better to be alone than with bad company.

❖

Children must learn to enjoy being alone. Throughout their lives, your children will have periods of alone time. If they learn how to handle solitude now it won't be so shocking when they live on their own without immediate family support.

Principle #135

Teach your children the keys to stable friendships: honesty, sharing and giving.

---- ✳ ----

The relationships your children form throughout their lives will be stronger, more satisfying and will last longer if they practice these values from a young age.

Principle #136

Teach your children the phrase:
"Make new friends, but keep the old.
One is silver and the other gold!"

❋

Children are often attracted to what's new and cool, be it toys
or people. Teach your children to value both the new and the
old. Children who ignore longtime friends to play with new-
er ones may find themselves regarded as disloyal. Let them
know that the new friend may not necessarily stick around.

PRINCIPLE #137

Know where your children are at all times.

※

Although it may seem to bother them, this close contact will make your children feel secure. When other children know that your children are closely monitored, they will be less likely to propose risky behavior to them.

PRINCIPLE #138

Teach your children how to stand up against peer pressure.

— ❋ —

By following the principles in this book, you are doing the best you can to ensure that you remain the most important and positive influence in your children's lives. Work with your children and teach them the specific words and phrases that they can use in high-pressure situations.

PRINCIPLE #139

Remember that your children will be
tempted to follow their friends
good or bad behaviors.

Your children are attracted to people who share similar values
and interests. Nurture good values in your children from an
early age so that they will gravitate toward the right friends
throughout their lives.

PRINCIPLE #140

Keep criticisms to a minimum with teenagers.

※

If you constantly criticize and condemn your teenagers, they will listen to their peers rather than to you. Adolescence is a time of rebellion. If you treat your teenage children's ideas and choices with respect, they will be less likely to rebel against your values.

PRINCIPLE #141

Make sure your children know that your house rules apply to friends' and relatives' homes as well.

---- ✳ ----

A well-behaved child is welcome in any home. Their popularity with other parents and relatives will enhance their self-esteem.

DEVELOPING A SENSE
OF BELONGING

Social organization experts know that when the institution, family, corporation or church benefits the individual, its rules are followed. The individual develops "buy in" to the organization's philosophy and approach to life. Your child needs the same kind of "buy in" to abide by your rules and family structure. This can only happen when you devote the time, energy and attention to convince your children that they are central in your life. In other words, to get the respect, cooperation and love you need from your children, you have to invest your time and resources.

At the same time, your children need to have a sense of their own boundaries within the family. Children who are respected will be less likely to become defensive and battle limits perceived as constraining.

Belonging to a larger group is crucial for humans. Otherwise, we have the feeling we're "dying of loneliness." Our unconscious knows well that we cannot exist in isolation. Bears and cougars can. But humans as well as wolves, elephants and many other animals literally die when alienated from a social group. Deep down, our connection to others nourishes us as much as food. A successful child is an outgrowth of a successful family.

PRINCIPLE #142

Make time for fun family activities,
such as playing sports, baking cookies,
going to the park, the zoo,
museums or the movies.

Add fun activities to your family routine. Shape your children's perception of their family as their most interesting social circle. The more they enjoy being with their family, the more influence their family will have on them.

Principle #143

Capitalize on family identity.

·❊·

Discuss your family's positive traits so that your children will acquire them. Say things like, "The Smiths are hard-working," or "We McFarlands don't look down on those who have less than we do," to demonstrate your family's core values. Conversely, you can say, "The Clarks are not lazy!" to motivate your children to get their chores done.

PRINCIPLE #144

Carry photos of your children in your wallet or purse.

— ✳ —

This shows your children that you love them, are proud of them and that they are the most important parts of your life.

PRINCIPLE #145

The best birthday present you can give your children is to write each of them a letter recapping all the special things they did throughout the year.

---- ❋ ----

Recap your children's best moments as well as your thoughts and feelings. Read these letters aloud on their birthday, but then tuck them away. Give your children all these letters on their 30th birthday. They will cherish this gift for the rest of their lives. Family rituals like this help couples and families create a sense of belonging and closeness that fosters relationships.

PRINCIPLE #146

If you love and respect your children
when they are young, they will
love you when you are old.

Conversely, if you fail to show love and respect to your children, they will not feel the obligation to care for you as you grow older. They will not have that debt of gratitude. If you sacrifice for them, it will make a lasting impression.

PRINCIPLE #147

Take a formal picture of the whole family every year.

---- ❋ ----

These will become great memories in the years ahead as the whole family grows together. Keep the file as well as several copies of each picture so you can give a complete set to each of your children on their 30th birthday. Your children will get a kick out of seeing how they've grown up over the years. Yearly photos also constitute a family ritual and promote family unity.

PRINCIPLE #148

Develop family rituals around the holidays.

— ✳ —

If you're looking for ideas, go to your parents and grandparents to find out what they did or what those of your nationality typically do for each of the major holidays. You can also find information about fun holiday rituals on the Internet or in books. Allow your children to help decide which ideas to try.

PRINCIPLE #149

Get involved in your children's activities.

--- ✳ ---

When you're volunteering at your children's school, leading Scouts or coaching a sports team, you can more easily monitor your children's behavior and whom they've chosen as friends. Sacrificing your time to be involved with your children will convince them that they really are first in your life. It has been proven in study after study that uninvolved or negligent parents have children more likely to get into trouble.

PRINCIPLE #150

Encourage your children to spend time together.

———————— ❈ ————————

Although siblings can develop rivalries, they can also be valuable support and role models for one another, especially later in life.

DEVELOPING SELF-MOTIVATION

It's human nature to forget to compliment someone on a job well done. It's also human nature to bring up any and every complaint. Let your children know, before they leave home, that the world reacts more strongly to their negative actions and simply absorbs their positive ones. It's a hard lesson to learn. Because society can react negatively to your children, it's crucial that they have their family as a cheering team.

More important, however, is our children's ability to motivate themselves to be the best workers, parents or community members they can be. It can be difficult to remember that success requires a great deal of failure as young people discover their own capabilities. Your children can be very hard on themselves. Stress to them that just because something isn't the best, it doesn't mean it isn't good.

If our children can learn to self-motivate, they will be immune to the criticisms of people who have their own agendas—and most people do. Once you impress upon your child to express their talents and skills for the benefit of those around them and society in general, they won't feel so self-conscious.

Principle #151

Teach your children that winners
focus on their successes rather
than their failures.

❋

Children must learn to concentrate on their achievements
and be proud of their accomplishments. If they can learn from
their failures and focus on their successes they will be more
likely to achieve their goals.

Principle #152

Give your children purpose in life
and they will flourish beyond
your expectations.

---- ❊ ----

Convince your children that they were born with a combination of skills no one else has. Tell them it's their duty to discover and develop these skills and put them to use for the benefit of society. Teach young children that they have a purpose in the smooth operation of the family as well.

Principle #153

If your child chooses a goal that does not seem to suit his or her temperament or skills, encourage him or her to try another activity.

❋

Remind your children that even though they did not succeed, they learned skills and knowledge that may help them in the pursuit of other goals. Reassure them that they will find their niche, and that failures are not a waste of time but part of the self-discovery process.

Principle #154

Work to take the words "I can't" out of your children's vocabulary.

---------------- ❊ ----------------

Instead, teach your children that they can achieve anything so long as they are willing to work hard to achieve it. The things most worth having are those that take incredible effort. Even failure should not dissuade them if their desire remains.

Principle #155

Think of yourself as your children's
permanent cheerleader.

✳

No matter how old they are, children can always benefit from
the support of a parent. Always applaud their best efforts.

Developing a Sense
of Spirituality

A need for something greater than ourselves exists in most of us. It's important for your children's identity that they be exposed to some form of spirituality or religion. Children take great comfort in thinking that something beyond their parents is looking out for them and loves them. They are also very curious about the world and why things happen. Religion provides some of these answers. You and your children can discuss exactly how much of your religious beliefs to follow. Eventually, your children will be able to delineate their own beliefs about the meaning of life. This knowledge will build confidence.

Religion can also provide a regular social outlet for families. It's difficult to consistently find ways to get together with others, especially when everyone is so busy. Church provides a structure to connect with other families and enjoy our own families during their events. Humans long to connect with others and feel a sense of community. If we cultivate a sense of spirituality in ourselves and our children, our families will benefit tremendously.

PRINCIPLE #156

Expose your children to religion, whatever religion you choose.

---　※　---

Believing in a higher power gives children a reason to do the right things, and attending religious services reminds them of the proper moral choices. Religion also helps children make sense of a chaotic world. Children in a Sunday school class or youth group may provide an alternate social circle to those at school. When things aren't going so well at school, your children will have their church friends to lean on for support and comfort.

Principle #157

Never expect your children to be perfect.

❋

Some children are born perfectionists. This trait drives them to do their best work, but it can also cause them great stress. Perfectionists are also less likely to try new things because they believe they will not succeed. Explaining that no one is perfect and, letting them know that it's okay to fail on occasion, encourages them to take risks.

PRINCIPLE #158

Encourage your children to help others less fortunate than they are.

※

When children see the day-to-day struggles of those in dire circumstances, they will appreciate what they have. Consider doing charity work together as a family. That way you can support your favorite cause, provide valuable lessons for your children, spend time with them and cultivate a common interest.

Principle #159

Get your children out into nature.

— ✳ —

Being outdoors helps children understand that they are part of a greater plan. Instill in them a sense of awe for the beautiful colors and patterns in trees, flowers and horizons. Your children will come to understand that they are amazing too!

PRINCIPLE #160

Encourage your children to sit in the first rows in school and in church.

---

* ✳ *

If they sit in the front rows, they will pay more attention to what the teacher or clergy is saying. Children who sit in the back rows are more likely to goof off and ignore important lessons.

PRINCIPLE #161

Teach your children that faith is crucial in dealing with life's challenges.

———————— ❊ ————————

When your children have faith in a higher power, it gives them hope in even the lowest moments of their life.

PRINCIPLE #162

Teach your children that one of their
purposes in life is to make the
world a better place.

--- ❋ ---

Explain to your children that everyone can make a difference.
Teach them that it's their duty as good people to put their
talents into helping others and adding value to the world
around them.

Principle #163

Encourage your children to volunteer to help others in need.

———————— ✳ ————————

This will give them a great feeling of importance and put their own concerns into perspective.

BECOMING A GOOD PARENT/TEACHER/CAREGIVER

The previous sections explain how to shape children's behavior and develop good values. The principles in the following sections mostly focus on how parents themselves should behave. No matter what we tell our children, it's our behavior that they absorb most. For that reason, we must make sure we're presenting a positive outlook and acting in a way that builds our children's strengths rather than diminishes them.

If you are struggling with maintaining a positive outlook or are having a hard time parenting, make sure to get some help. Counselors provide a place to blow off steam and can suggest strategies for your specific situation. Know, too, that all parents struggle with certain aspects of child rearing. It can seem like no other family has troubles to the extent that yours does, but that is simply not the case.

PRINCIPLE #164

Teach your children that the glass
is half full, not half empty.

---- ✳ ----

Every situation has pros and cons. Your children must learn
to focus on the good side of every situation rather than focusing on the negative side.

Principle #165

Don't make the mistake that most parents make. When their children are very young, parents concentrate on every step they take. When they are older, parents concentrate on every misstep they make.

———— ✳ ————

Although the accomplishments of young children, such as walking and talking, may seem more impressive, your older children's successes are just as important and should be recognized. Shaping behavior through praise is a lifelong endeavor.

PRINCIPLE #166

Take care of yourself.

---- ✳ ----

Rearing children is incredibly taxing. To do your best job, you must feel rested, strong and happy. Participate in some activities that reinforce your identity as an individual. If you take care of yourself, your children will want to take care of themselves too.

Principle #167

Don't expect your children to excel in sports, music, academics or even business just because you did.

Let them excel in whatever they so choose. Encourage your children's talents and accept their limitations. Set goals based on their abilities and interests. When children realize that you understand what they are made of and still love them, they will trust and love you even more.

Principle #168

Parenting cannot be scheduled.

———————————— ✳ ————————————

Life happens. You must be able to roll with the punches. This means you need to be a good teacher for your children on a full-time basis. You can't always plan for what's around the corner, but by keeping communication open and being consistent in your discipline, you will be more prepared for those situations that sneak up on you.

Principle #169

Give your children time to grow up
and mature. Only then will they
fulfill your expectations.

※

Children mature at different paces. Some may know their path
from birth: others may not discover their talents until much
later in life. The best thing you can do is give them a strong,
loving foundation from which their skills can spring forth
whenever they are ready.

PRINCIPLE #170

Be aware of the mood you regularly exhibit.

--- ❋ ---

Children absorb their parents' attitudes. Which behavior or attitude are your children getting from you? If your outlook is negative, your children will come to see the world in a negative light. Creativity and motivation is zapped by negative attitudes. Do your best to avoid negative language or pessimistic attitudes around your children.

Principle #171

Be vigilant to model the behavior you want your children to display.

——— ✳ ———

Experts claim that 90% of children's early behaviors come from their parents. Always behave as though your children are in the room with you so that positive behaviors become second nature.

PRINCIPLE #172

Remember that your children are watching you closely.

━━━━━━━━━━━━━━━ ❋ ━━━━━━━━━━━━━━━

Your children will not listen to your directions if you act in a hypocritical way. Remember that actions speak louder than words. Do not fall into the bad habit of telling children to "do as I say, not as I do."

Principle #173

Remember that what you do will have more influence on your children than what you say.

✳

Children will follow the behavior of their parents, no matter what their parents teach them. Words they hear have much less power than the actions they see.

Principle #174

Don't give the message to your children
that rules are made to be kept by
children but broken by parents.

---- ❋ ----

This double standard will teach your children that when they
grow up, they can break all the rules and it won't matter.
They will also perceive the double standard as unfair.

PRINCIPLE #175

Never argue aggressively with your spouse in front of your children.

Reserve this kind of situation for when the two of you are alone. Children often feel their parents' disagreements are their fault, a misconception that can torpedo their self-esteem and make them feel unsafe.

Principle #176

It's okay to resolve issues with your
spouse in front of your children
as long as it is conducted in a
civilized manner.

❋

This is how they will learn to resolve conflicts with others.
Do not yell at or belittle your spouse. Listen to his or her concerns and respond in a thoughtful manner. Remember that certain issues are inappropriate for a child to hear. Conduct those types of discussions in private.

PRINCIPLE #177

Agree on a disciplinary strategy
with your spouse and stick
to your plan.

✳

Children feel secure when the messages you give them are consistent. When children are confused about limits, they will test you to see what they can get away with. If parents don't present a unified front, children will learn how to manipulate and play one parent against the other.

PRINCIPLE #178

Don't spoil your children's childhood fantasies like Santa Claus, the Easter Bunny and the Tooth Fairy.

This imaginative phase is crucial to your children's development. Don't be the ones to discourage their imagination. Nurture their sense of wonder and magic as long as you can.

Principle #179

When the Tooth Fairy leaves money after picking up a tooth, have her leave a little note for your child.

---- ✳ ----

Letters from Santa Claus and the Easter Bunny are also great reinforcements. These notes should tell your children how good they have been and encourage them to keep up the good work. Hearing this from someone they look up to and respect, aside from their parents, will encourage your children to be good.

PRINCIPLE #180

As often as possible, try to have
one-on-one time with each
of your children.

※

This time together strengthens the bond between you and
your children. It also proves to your children that they are
valuable enough to merit your undivided attention.

Principle #181

Teach your children to appreciate and be happy with what they have or receive.

Children who get used to always getting more or better toys, clothes or electronic gadgets rarely feel satisfied. While our consumer culture makes it difficult to move our children's focus from material things, try to emphasize the real joys in life: friendship, a safe home, and the expression of their talents.

PRINCIPLE #182

Read this book, read it often, and read it over and over again!

---   ✳   ---

You and your spouse should read this book often. Give a copy of this book to other family members and parents of your children's friends. Impress upon them that there is a great deal to know about children that will make parenting easier and more enjoyable. If you share your thoughts and struggles with other parents, you can provide better support to one another when dealing with the challenges of parenthood.

Principle #183

If your child has a specific issue like ADHD* or dyslexia, research and read the best books on the topic.

---- ❊ ----

Maternal and paternal instincts only go so far. A significant portion of our tax dollars go into researching the best ways to address and resolve our children's medical and psychological issues. Not only will you find specific strategies to help your situation, but you can also find support groups that will give you the strength to tackle the issues. When parenting is not simple, arm yourself with information.

* Attention Deficit Hyperactivity Disorder

Principle #184

If men are from Mars and women are from Venus, then children are from Jupiter.

---　✳　---

Just as there are serious physiological differences between the minds of men and women, there are serious physiological differences between the adult, teen, and adolescent brain. The neurons in the human mind are not fully covered, or *myelinated*, until one reaches 31 years of age. This means the brain is not fully organized or operating at capacity until then. Be confident that once your children become adults, you will understand each other better.

PRINCIPLE #185

Stimulate all five of your children's senses in the early years.

———————— ❋ ————————

During the first year of life, 70-80% of all brain cells will be completely developed. At no other time in life does the brain master so many skills. In the next few years, vocabulary, math and logic skills are largely determined and emotional stability is greatly affected. The brain actually pares down or "kills off" neurons that are not used regularly. Make sure to get as many of those neurons engaged as possible by talking to your babies, showing them stimulating objects, letting them feel different textures, smell different scents and taste all kinds of flavors.

Principle #186

Don't focus too much attention on your children's problems.

---- ✳ ----

The more you focus on your children's problems, the bigger they become. Remind yourself that dealing with problems is part of growing up. Solving problems is a must-have quality to succeed in life.

PRINCIPLE #187

Raise your children with the qualities they need to succeed.

---- ❋ ----

The essential building blocks for success are problem-solving skills, a strong work ethic, creativity and integrity. These qualities will help your children be successful throughout their lives, in school, the workplace and at home. If your children have these abilities as adults, you will know that you have done a great job as a parent.

PRINCIPLE #188

Do not introduce your children as "shy" people.

✳

If you do, you reinforce a part of your children's identity that is best diminished. If you introduce your children as fun and friendly, they will become more outgoing and socially confident. Remember, what you say can become a self-fulfilling prophecy. Your children tend to live up to your expectations.

PRINCIPLE #189

Share your feelings with your children.

❋

Show your children it is fine for adults and children alike to express feelings of sadness and anger with each other. Indeed, this is the only way these feelings get resolved. Teach your children appropriate ways of expressing these emotions.

PRINCIPLE #190

Enjoy your children while they are young.

※

Really enjoy them—every word they say, every gesture they make, every funny thing they say or do. Children have a way of looking at the world that is special and cannot be replicated by adults. Consider keeping a journal and jotting down your children's comments and behaviors so that you can relive them later. These memories will bring you great joy.

Principle #191

You only get one chance at parenting a child. Give it your best shot.

---　❋　---

Think of parenting as a career for which you need to educate yourself, train and then perform to the best of your ability. Reward yourself when you know you've done a good job. Your efforts will be rewarded many times over when your children grow into adults who make you proud.

PRINCIPLE #192

Evaluate yourself as a parent on a daily basis.

---- ❊ ----

At the end of each day, ask yourself, "What did I do today to make my children better people?" and, "What message of love did I give my children today?"

PRINCIPLE #193

Apologize to your children when you make a mistake.

———————————— ❋ ————————————

Learning how to listen to your children, talk to them and respond to their actions does not always go without a hitch. When you make mistakes, as all parents do, it's fine to apologize to your children. Teach your children that everyone makes mistakes—even you! This will give your children a realistic view of humankind and bring you closer to one another.

Principle #194

Find things you like to do with your children.

---- ❋ ----

Your children will greatly appreciate and remember the time spent together. This will help you stay connected to your children and understand each other better.

PRINCIPLE #195

When things are tough for you,
avoid acting out angrily
toward your children.

---------------------------- ❋ ----------------------------

Children can frustrate us enough when our moods and life situations are stable. So when we are tense it becomes much easier for our children to set us off. If you feel you can't control your emotions in front of your children, find counseling and support with friends and professionals. Be careful not to take your bad day out on your children. Ask yourself this question, "Are their actions really that bad, or is my mood affecting my judgement?"

Principle #196

Relate and connect with your children the way you wish your parents would have done with you.

---- ✳ ----

Don't assume your parents knew what they were doing. If you learn new and better ways to relate to your children, use them. Try to be conscious of which of your parents' behavior was most difficult for you as a child. Be attuned to whether you are doing the same. It is easy for parents to fall into the same patterns as their own parents did.

PRINCIPLE #197

When you are with your children, focus on the beauty of the moment.

———————— ❈ ————————

Just concentrate on your children. Forget about work, other relationships, and incomplete household tasks. Consider hiring out some of the more tedious housework if you're constantly distracted by it. Your children can tell if you are distracted, and they might feel that you do not enjoy the time you spend with them.

PRINCIPLE #198

Use the "Simple Principles" not
only for young children, but
for teenagers as well.

✳

Don't think that your parenting tasks are completed just because your children have reached the teen years. As teenagers prepare to graduate from high school and enter college
or the workforce, their greatest challenges lie ahead of them.
They need your support now as much as ever. These "Simple
Principles" will be crucial during this period of development
as well.

Principle #199

Remember that your children are the promise and hope for the future.

※

You have a heavy responsibility to guarantee that you're putting into society young adults who can empathize with others, work to their best abilities, and nurture their loved ones. If you succeed, the world will be enhanced by the fruit of your efforts. You will also experience the greatest satisfaction humans can achieve.

Principle #200

Teach your children to respect the elderly.

---— ✳ —---

The elderly have a great deal to teach our children. They help children gain perspective on life. Their life's accomplishments should be valued. Also, if they don't learn to respect the elderly, they won't respect you when you get old.

WORDS TO PRAISE
YOUR CHILDREN

This section lists some examples of positive words you can say to reinforce your child's good behavior. Acknowledging your children's good behavior with positive words will strengthen their desire for your approval. They will be more likely to follow rules and will learn to compliment others.

A+ Job
Amazing
Awesome
Astounding

Beautiful
Beautiful Work
Bingo
Bravo

Breathtaking
Brilliant

Congratulations
Cool

Dazzling
Delightful
Dynamite

Excellent
Excellent Job

Fabulous
Fantastic
Fantastic Job

Good
Good for You
Good Job
Gorgeous
Grand
Great
Great Discovery

Hip Hip Hooray
Hooray for You
Hot Dog
How Nice

How Smart
How Wonderful

I Knew You Could Do It
I Like You
I Love It When You Laugh
I Love the Way You Are
I Love You
I Love Your Smile
Impressive
I'm Proud of You
Incredible
Ingenious
I Respect You
I Trust You

Looking Good
Looks Great

Magnificent
Marvelous
My Buddy

Nice Try
Nice Work
Now You've Got It
Now You're Flying

Out-of-this-World
Outstanding
Outstanding Performance

Perfect
Phenomenal
Pretty Good

Really Great
Remarkable

Remarkable Job
Sensational
Spectacular
Splendid
Stupendous
Super
Super Job
Super Star
Super Work

Terrific
That's My Boy/Girl
That's the Best
That's Incredible
Top Rate

Unbelievable

Very Good
Very Nice

Way to Go
Well Done
What a Good Listener
What an Imagination
Wonderful
Wow

You're Exciting
You're Fantastic
You're Fun
You're Growing Up
You're Important
You're Important to Me
You're Incredible
You're My Friend
You're on Target

You're on Top of It
You're on Your Way
You're Okay
You're Smart
You Brighten My Day
You Care
You Did It
You Figured It Out
You Learned It Well
You Make Me Happy
You Make Me Laugh
You Make My Day
You Mean a Lot to Me
You Tried Hard
You're a Good Friend
You're a Good Student
You're a Joy
You're a Real Trooper
You're a Treasure

You're a Winner
You're Awesome
You're Beautiful
You're Catching On
You're Darling
You're Doing Great
You're Perfect
You're Precious
You're Responsible
You're Sensational
You're So Lucky
You're Special
You're Spectacular
You're Terrific
You're Unique
You're Wonderful
You've Got a Friend

Questions to Ask Your Children

Asking questions is an important part of maintaining good communication with your children. This section lists some examples of questions you should ask your children in different scenarios. These questions can help to open up a dialogue and show them that you are interested in their lives. Listening to their response lets them know that they are important and that you respect them.

Questions to Ask Your Children...
- After School
- During Dinner
- In the Morning
- During an Emotional Situation
- To Improve Their Self-Esteem
- About Safety

Questions to Ask Yourself

Questions to Ask Your Children After School

- What do you like best about your school?
- What do you like least about your school?
- What did you do for fun at school today?
- What is the hardest thing for you at school?
- Who did you play with today?
- What did your teacher think about your homework?
- How did you do on your test?
- What do you like the best about this friend?
- Why does this friend make you feel special?
- What is the coolest thing you learned today?
- Why do you think your teacher reprimanded you?
- What could you have done to avoid that argument?
- What is the best way to help you understand?
- How did you feel when you got an A on your test?
- How did you feel when you got an F on your test?
- How would you feel if you got the best grade?
- How would you feel if you got first place?

Questions to Ask Your Children During Dinner

- What is the best thing that happened to you today?
- What is the coolest thing that happened to you today?
- What did you do today that you are proud of?
- What did you do today that you wish you had not done?
- What do you like the best about your family?
- What do you like the least about your family?
- What are you looking forward to tomorrow?
- What are you looking forward to next week?
- What would you like to do this weekend?
- What are you looking forward to doing when you grow up?
- Where would you like to go on vacation?
- What's your favorite thing about school?
- What is your favorite thing to do after school?
- What would you like to learn more about?
- What do you want to be when you grow up?
- What do you think you have to do to accomplish that?
- How should we divide the chores?

QUESTIONS TO ASK YOUR CHILDREN IN THE MORNING

- Who are you going to play with today?
- What are you looking forward to today?
- Do you feel confident about your test/homework?
- Did you get a good night's sleep?
- What are you looking forward to doing in school today?
- What do you like the best about yourself today?
- What can you do to make today a special day?
- What do you like the most about your friends?
- What do you like the most about your teacher?
- What would you like to do after school today?
- Who would you like to invite over to play with you?

Questions to Ask Your Children During an Emotional Situation

- How do you think we should handle this?
- What would you do if you were the parent?
- What is the lesson to be learned from this situation?
- Why do you think you're being punished?
- What punishment do you think you deserve?
- What do you think is the most important thing about this episode?
- How did you feel about that decision?
- What should you have done in this situation?
- How do you think so-and-so would feel in this situation?
- Who should you have turned to for help?
- Where could you have gone to find help?
- How can you avoid this situation in the future?

Questions to Ask Your Children to Improve Their Self-Esteem

- What other ways could we solve this problem?
- Will you teach me how to do that?
- Could you show me how you do that?
- What should I do in this situation?
- What would you do if you were me?
- What is the best way to handle this?
- Do you think your father/mother could do that?
- How in the world did you make that move?
- What do you think we should do?
- Can you believe you did that?
- How did you learn to do that?
- What pleases you the most about your performance?
- What do you like the most about yourself?
- Why do you think you are so popular at school?
- Why do you think you are such a great athlete?
- Why do you think you are such a good student?

Questions to Ask Your Children About Safety

What Would You Do If . . . ?

- a stranger offered you a ride home from school?
- you came home and saw a stranger inside the house?
- your sister/brother was hurt and there were no adults nearby?
- there was a fire in the kitchen?
- a friend offered you a cigarette?
- a friend asked you to do something you consider wrong?
- you got lost in the theater/mall and I could not find you?
- your friends were stealing things from a store?
- your friends asked you to steal from a store?
- you saw an older child abusing a younger one?
- your car got a flat tire?
- someone knocked on your door late at night?
- someone asked you to lie for them?
- you needed to call home but didn't have any money or a cell phone?
- I got injured and no other adult was around?

Questions to Ask Yourself

- How can I get closer to my children?
- What can I do today to show my love for them?
- What can I do today to improve any unresolved issues?
- Why are my children special to me?
- What would I do if something were to happen to my children?
- What would happen to my children if I were no longer around?
- Am I doing the best for my children?
- How can I be the most helpful to my children right now?
- How can I get my children to understand me better?
- How can I understand my children better?
- How often do I criticize my child?
- How often do I provide specific, positive feedback?
- Do I encourage pride, enthusiasm and confidence in my children?

CONCLUSION

In many ways, parenting has never been more difficult than it is in the 21st century. Parents must guard children against the negative messages and risky opportunities that come their way, making child-rearing far more complex and confusing than it has ever been.

Child-rearing gurus tear apart each other's strategies in the media. One theory comes out only to be contradicted the next month. But often they are not much help or helpful in every situation. For parents, trying to determine which approach will create the happiest, most successful children can be exasperating.

Finally, *Simple Principles to Raise a Successful Child* provides a distillation of parenting advice that will effectively create happy families and successful children no matter the social status or parenting style. Use it and watch your family connect and grow stronger. Not only will you benefit but you'll also be doing a great service to society.

The United States has gone far enough in pushing the prominence of the "individual." It is time to return to an emphasis on family connections. It's imperative that society put family first again. When that happens, individuals, families and society at large will enjoy a renaissance that has been long overdue.